DATE DUE

Dogs

Poodles

by Lisa Trumbauer

Consulting Editor: Gail Saunders-Smith, PhD

Consultant: Jennifer Zablotny, DVM
Member, American Veterinary Medical Association

Capstone
press
Mankato, Minnesota

Pebble Books are published by Capstone Press,
151 Good Counsel Drive, P.O. Box 669, Mankato, Minnesota 56002.
www.capstonepress.com

1 2 3 4 5 6 11 10 09 08 07 06

Library of Congress Cataloging-in-Publication Data
Trumbauer, Lisa, 1963–
    Poodles / by Lisa Trumbauer.
    p. cm—(Pebble Books. Dogs)
    Summary: "Simple text and photographs present an introduction to the poodle
breed, its growth from puppy to adult, and pet care information"—Provided by
publisher.
    Includes bibliographical references and index.
    ISBN-13: 978-0-7368-5335-4 (hardcover)
    ISBN-10: 0-7368-5335-9 (hardcover)
    1. Poodles—Juvenile literature. I. Title. II. Series.
SF429.P85T78 2006
636.72'8—dc22   2005021596

Note to Parents and Teachers

The Dogs set supports national science standards related to life
science. This book describes and illustrates poodles. The images
support early readers in understanding the text. The repetition of
words and phrases helps early readers learn new words. This book
also introduces early readers to subject-specific vocabulary words,
which are defined in the Glossary section. Early readers may need
assistance to read some words and to use the Table of Contents,
Glossary, Read More, Internet Sites, and Index sections of the book.

Table of Contents

4

Show Dogs

Poodles are show dogs.
Poodles with fancy haircuts
compete against other
dogs in dog shows.

Poodles work hard
at dog shows.
They jump and do tricks.

From Puppy to Adult

Three to five puppies
are born
in each poodle litter.

Poodle puppies are smart.
They play and learn
together as they grow.

Adult poodles come
in three sizes.
Toy poodles are small.
Standard poodles are big.
Miniature poodles are
in between.

Poodle Care

Poodles need
dog food, fresh water,
and walks every day.

A poodle's curly fur is always growing. Poodles need haircuts every two months.

18

Poodle fur can get
matted and tangled.
Owners must brush
their poodles often.

Poodles are smart, active dogs.
Love and care make poodles happy pets.

Glossary

active—busy and full of energy

compete—to try hard to do better than others at a task, race, or contest

dog show—a contest where judges pick the best dog in several events

litter—a group of animals born at one time to the same mother

matted—stuck together

tangled—twisted together in a confused group

Read More

Fitzpatrick, Anne. *Poodles.* Mankato, Minn.: Smart Apple Media, 2003.

Stone, Lynn M. *Poodles.* Eye to Eye with Dogs. Vero Beach, Fla.: Rourke, 2003.

Internet Sites

FactHound offers a safe, fun way to find Internet sites related to this book. All of the sites on FactHound have been researched by our staff.

Here's how:

1. Visit *www.facthound.com*

2. Type in this special code **0736853359** for age-appropriate sites. Or enter a search word related to this book for a more general search.

3. Click on the **Fetch It** button.

FactHound will fetch the best sites for you!

Index

Word Count: 115
Grade: 1
Early-Intervention Level: 13

Editorial Credits
Martha E. H. Rustad, editor; Juliette Peters, designer; Kelly Garvin, photo researcher;
Scott Thoms, photo editor

Photo Credits
Ardea/Jean Paul Ferrero, 8; Cheryl A. Ertelt, 18; Corbis/Tom Stewart, 20; Elite Portrait
Design/Lisa Fallenstein-Holthaus, 14, 16; Kent Dannen, cover, 10, 12; Mark Raycroft, 1;
Mira/Karen Stewart, 6; Zuma Press/Baron Catskill, 4